HOME IS A HEART THAT FLEES
NURAIN ỌLÁDÈJÌ

This is a work of fiction. All names, characters, places, and incidents are a product of the author's imagination. Any resemblance to real events or persons, living or dead, is entirely coincidental.

Published by Akashic Books
©2024 Nurain Ọládèjì
ISBN: 978-1-63614-217-3

All rights reserved
Printed in China
First printing

Akashic Books
Instagram, X, Facebook: AkashicBooks
info@akashicbooks.com
www.akashicbooks.com

African Poetry Book Fund
Prairie Schooner
University of Nebraska
110 Andrews Hall
Lincoln, Nebraska 68588

TABLE OF CONTENTS

Preface by Tyree Daye 4

Facing East 8
A Bowl of Moonlight 9
Puppy in Love 11
Crawling West 12
My Father Renamed Himself 13
Our Muezzin Is an Ocean 14
An Audience Learns the Plot 16
The Statesman 17
Mercy 19
Everything Breaks 20
A Boy's Self-Appraisal 21
Wiping the Sky 22
The Moment before Impact 23
A Light-Rail That Derailed 24
Extended Incubation 25
Considering Silence 26
Collateral Damage 27
The Function of Eyes 28
Dying Chemically 29
Home Is a Heart That Flees 30

Acknowledgments 32

PREFACE
by Tyree Daye

The speaker of Nurain Ọládèjì's *Home Is a Heart That Flees* seems to have a familiar dilemma; they live in a country that needs them but does not want them. Their home is the only home they have, even when it sometimes tries to kill them, and if they were to leave, no matter where they decided to live, they would only be a visitor:

> Here we must lie on infested
>
> beds without sheets, but to go elsewhere
> is to be reminded that in a hotel, you can
> only be a guest.
> ("Home Is a Heart That Flees")

The opening poem, "Facing East," shows the complications of living in a world-dominating capitalist system.

> I claw my way up to break through the surface
> of an oil stream. I am lost in my own parable.
> Let me feel my way back to my father's voice.

When the day is over, the speaker has time to think outside of the capitalist mindset, so they turn east toward the sun.

> I turn in thoughts at dawn
> toward the sun because I have used up my ration
> of words, and now I fail at the ultimate language

As a result of enjambment, the word *ration* starts as a set amount of something valuable, then refers to words themselves. Being out of words, the speaker fails to speak the "ultimate" language of the world, which is money. The speaker of these poems lives in dueling mentalities. In the effects of social and political unrest, they "have not seen the flames [. . . but] have been burned." They crawl through oil as they try to move closer to what is burning them.

In poems such as "Crawling West," the speaker describes "crawling toward a sunset." The speaker is worried that they have nothing to give and that their:

> wounds grow into
> one another because there isn't enough light
>
> in which to cast the whole of a life.

However, the speaker sees the struggle toward the West as a necessary undertaking:

> but I must
> continue to stretch them forth so I don't
> end up with nothing to give you, or myself.

"Facing East" and "Crawling West" are the dueling mentalities manifested in these poems. The speaker writes in "Facing East":

> I turn to face east; everywhere else leads away
> from truth. I know because I followed each road
> but had to turn and walk back to what I already know.

We are invited to live in the parable with a speaker who has left home, but who lives in the memory of home while trying to honor the ancestral. These poems embrace the beautiful risk of sentimentality. Our hearts are allowed to be their fully articulate selves. These poems are crafted with lyrical bursts that push and complicate the narrative, presenting a duality of choices. Neither of these choices are easy.

> You will let them kill you, but you'll find
> this death is a ticket to nirvana: a cascade
> where your dreams, having edited your
> memories, crash into one another and slide off,
> smoothening cracks in your memory,
> glossing over ruins on the portrait of your
> imagined future.
> ("Dying Chemically")

Ọládèjì asks the essential questions of what success means. Why does success so often take us away from the people we love? In the final poem of *Home Is a Heart That Flees,* Ọládèjì brings these questions to a boil:

> Home is to where the heart flees.
> When each of us who bear scars of our
> country's stabs sleeps, we fly over
> the Atlantic and its siblings into dreams.

In sleep is where the speaker of *Home Is a Heart That Flees* finds comfort while remaining in the place that raised them. Ọládèjì complicates the word *dreams*—they are dreams that come with sleep and the dreams we have for our lives.

I am moved by the work of Nurain Ọládèjì, for the ways in which he challenges his own sense of the world and wrestles with the complexes of success and failure as an artist. A part of me is further engaged by the poet because I too live in a country that needs me but does not want me. Ọládèjì reminds us that the answer to such dilemmas of identity are found in poetry—in its beauty and honesty.

FACING EAST

I turn to face east; everywhere else leads away
from truth. I know because I followed each road
but had to turn and walk back to what I already know.

Perhaps I am not my father's son. I have not lost
my country, it is the seeds that fail to sprout greens.
They made new ways to speed us through to the end

of days, but we, resolute in our amplified ego,
are buoyed by the certainty that only half
of us will drown. I turn in thoughts at dawn

toward the sun because I have used up my ration
of words, and now I fail at the ultimate language
the world speaks. The world does not need

a savior; its glory is in never failing to find
equilibrium. We have carved eyes for a storm that
has never had much use for direction. I have not

seen the flames; I have not smelled the smoke;
yet, I have been burned. If I can't go ahead, I can
at least turn around. But, submerged by its density,

I claw my way up to break through the surface
of an oil stream. I am lost in my own parable.
Let me feel my way back to my father's voice.

A BOWL OF MOONLIGHT

I awake a stranger to your silence.
I am lying on my side, gazing out through
our bedroom window. It is a half-moon tonight,

a bowl of half-light sitting on the night sky.
Milk-white light fills our room as mourners had
filled the living room. I turn on my side and the moon,

through the perfect rectangle of our window, cuts
my shadow off at the chest. I want to remember this
like a personal message from God, saying

*I cannot be there with you, but I have not left you
all by yourself.* I want to remember this silence
and this room and this moon and this wall

and this fresh wakefulness. I turn back: the moon
is still there, but it has taken steps back. I think nothing
of this. I am too alone to think anything of this.

I have feasted to my fill and did not notice the bowl
was emptying. The half-light is rising or dropping.
I turn to the wall again and my shadow is smudging,

like our home now. I do not return my gaze
to the window. I know the table has been cleared.
The moon, like you, has shrouded itself in clouds,

like the last of mourners who had slipped out through the back. They must have figured that, now, a bereaved must loathe goodbyes.

PUPPY IN LOVE

My roommate brought it home
nine weeks ago—a puppy, wet eyed
and uninitiated in the nuance of affection,
trudging after everyone, running after
our neighbor's children, whose screams
must have seemed to it like a call to play,
a love reciprocated. It would wag its tail
and trudge after me when I passed, trying to smell
my feet. I would turn and scowl,
even kicking it one day when my mood was foul.

It keeps its distance now.
With new wisdom, it sits and stares at me like
a helpless lover—face drooping, tail up,
eyes on the verge of tears. And a small—
very small—part of me wants to kneel beside it,
rest its head on my lap and tickle its neck.
I walk away wondering if this being
with love spilling over would ever learn that
the greatest lie ever told about love
is that it sets you free.

CRAWLING WEST

May whoever hurt me, forgive me.
—*Adélia Prado*

Perhaps I'd arrived late at my own birth.
I have been late all my life so it must have
begun somewhere. Amber-soaked clouds,
a last sight of a sun dying out, remind me

I am crawling toward a sunset with nothing
to take with me or leave behind. Even on my knees,
crawling, bleeding into earth, emptying myself
of desire and despair in equal measure, I have not

made a single plant grow an extra leaf.
I have nothing to give. Darkness weighs heavier
than light, so I know now that wounds grow into
one another because there isn't enough light

in which to cast the whole of a life. My palms
collect emptiness when I retract them, but I must
continue to stretch them forth so I don't
end up with nothing to give you, or myself.

MY FATHER RENAMED HIMSELF

A child's need to be chased, to hide and be found
time and again, is why my father is the ghost stalking
my waking dreams. When I was a child, hunting for

where to hide and wait for my friends to seek
me out, I found, inside an abandoned yard with
an unfinished building, a hole in the ground.

Something I do not know stopped me from jumping
into the hole, slowed me to stop at its edge and crane
my neck to watch the hole sink deeper; till I saw

ripples as the pebbles my feet had kicked touched
the water. Later, when my friends found me elsewhere,
I did not make a point of how I could have won this

game by ending it. I was named after a grieving lover
who then married his dead lover's sister, and on this
basis earned the title of *The Bearer of Double Lights*.

And when, again, his new lover died, he must have
learned that some lights are not bound by affection
to enliven man. When my father named me, he could not

have imagined that each of our worlds would be as
committed to resisting a convergence, he could not have
known that, naming me, he was only renaming himself.

OUR MUEZZIN IS AN OCEAN

1.

Our muezzin does not sing, his wheels run over
everything we know as song; a batologist pulling
flesh from syllables until we are sure they will break,

but they never do. They ooze out of speakers
and converge at the masjid's center. And when
he frees them, they explode into fireballs scorching

holes in our souls. His last line is a water molecule
which, having journeyed for a lifetime through pipes,
finds peace as a trickle from a faucet.

2.

Our muezzin calls and you hear him
with all your body. He pulls you into an abyss
of prayer, his hands over his ears as though

shielding himself from the weight of his own call.
He pushes you to the edge and when you are
about to fall off, you hear a crack,

the first of yourself about to be spilled,
just then, he relaxes. Your body realigns into
a new form molded by our muezzin.

3.

Our muezzin is an ocean. His waves, like
a cold drink, burn throats already laced
with menthol. He is a sun, his light swallowed

by those willing to pull out of their skin and climb
to a peak against sentry winds hauling shadows
into their eyes. Because we fail at agreement,

everything is right and wrong all at once,
and the muezzin's calls remain furled in words
lost within the grandness of memory.

AN AUDIENCE LEARNS THE PLOT

I did not arrive here by chance nor choose the valley
into which my path emptied. Since I did not have

what I would have wanted, I had tried to contain
myself within an idea that what is true is what refuses

to stay buried. I have lived long enough to accept,
to be an erratic anthology of all I've ever sensed,

an audience of Earth's narrative. Now I know that
whatever geography gives, sociology steals,

and I have grown dizzy trying to lock in a target
with my finger on whom to assign blame. This is why

I have resolved to choose the bullets I let
breach my skin. This is why I now preach that

since all of us climbed out of the same cave, no one
can be trusted to bridge our distance from dreams.

THE STATESMAN

The world would rather see hope than just hear
its song. And that's why statesmen have to smile.
—Wisława Szymborska

Morning after the governor lost reelection,
I returned to the capital. There was wind
after the rain in the little hours before sunrise;
and the thrill of yesterday failed to spill
into this Sunday. The bus stopped beside
a small bush for a passenger to disembark.
I watched small snails breaking past
the boundaries of bushes, pulling out to feel
the coolness of mud and tarmac.
The passenger, trying to control the chaos
that was his luggage, will never know
he had crushed one under his foot.

We drove deeper into the capital, into an assault
of the governor's face wailing at us from all sides.
Here, in purple T-shirt, shaven, he meant to look
youthful. And here, bright in matching helmet
and reflective jacket, arms folded across his
chest, he meant to show he's hands-on.
And here and here and also here, in lush colors
of agbada, he was gallant and pensive and playful
and I-don't-know-what-he's-trying-to-be-here.
Always in those large eyeglasses and sagging
cheeks, he wore a fixed savior-of-the-people smile.

All that ubiquity and the people still looked away.
Already I saw past the rainy and dry seasons ahead.
I watched the sun lick life out of the governor's faces,
the rains smudging them. And the churches, as the years
trickle out, will pull down what is left to make room.

MERCY

The rain had seized when I left the lab. The wind
eased me into its wrap, sending a chill into my scalp,
and I felt my hunger wilt. I had not received a text
from my bank yet, so I called my friend to ask if he had
sent the money. He said he had. I thanked him
and promised to pay back soon. People hurried past me
trying to reach safety before the rain would resume.
Standing all day to separate two hundred corn plants
into parts and then recording the weight of each part
in my notebook, I could only trudge through security
at the gate. Once out, I removed my Research Fellow ID
and stuffed it into my backpack. My stomach groaned.
I started to collect another round of saliva in my mouth
to swallow. I felt my phone vibrate. When I pulled it out,
the text turned out to have been imagined. It started to drizzle
and I tilted my head to the side to sneak water into my mouth.
People had filled the shade at the bus stop when I arrived.
I leaned against a pole at the shade's edge. I ignored the buses
that stopped—all I had was a fare for one bus trip; I could not
risk alighting at the bank only to collapse walking the rest
of the way home because I didn't have enough from which
the ATM could hand me. I checked my phone again.
The rain had picked up and I was promptly drenched.
The cold stung me but I was too tired to be aggrieved.
I left my mouth ajar, discretely swallowing water. It was when
I started to fear my phone would drown in my pocket that
I felt it vibrate. I pulled it out just enough to see that the text
was from the bank. I looked back up, grateful for the rain,
because now I can let the tears have their way.

EVERYTHING BREAKS

If a man has fallen in diverse ways,
pushed down enough times,
it is inevitable he'd have mastered
his maneuvers so that landing would not
break anything that would keep him
from rising back to his feet. He would have
mastered his breathing so that his lungs
would not collapse with every wind
knocked out of him.

And because he has achieved such a level
of mastery, he'd call to himself,
at one point, a force of a particular
magnitude that would hit him at a specific
angle at a precise time, such that this
would leave the tinniest of cracks
in his thickest bone. A wave would slip
through this crack, reach his center, and upset
a silence there that had never been rattled.

A BOY'S SELF-APPRAISAL

The boy arches his back and slumps his shoulders,
this means he lets himself be molded
by his spirit. If you own a body, are you liable
for actions of the spirit housed inside that body?
The boy's legs do not stride with vitality.
This morning, with the harmattan wind carrying
its message of dust and dryness, his eyes study
his feet and the ground holding them. His face jerks up
towards a window from where a face reveals itself
through parted curtains, looking elsewhere then
turning to settle on the boy with a smile—warm like
freshly served oatmeal. Oval, the shade of perfectly
roasted groundnut, it is a face which has kept him awake
at nights since kindergarten. The boy snatches away
with renewed devotion on studying his feet as though
nothing else is worthy of inquiry. He studies the dry
whiteness of his feet, the crookedness of his toenails.
He sees his face as he'd seen it earlier in the mirror—
an oblong mass assaulted by pimples. What is a boy worth,
he wonders, with his arched back and slumped shoulders,
if he is unworthy of accepting a serving of warm oatmeal.

WIPING THE SKY
after Seamus Heaney

In the day, when a rain winds down,
and the air is damp and the sky glooms,

it's like a child transitioning from a bawl
into sleep. And then, in an unfurling, the fog begins

to clear; the air sheds its weight. The sun returns
to a new sky, clear, wiped clean like glass.

If then, my dear, we sometimes find clouds
converging above us, the air between us dragging

under a new weight, we may watch the rain fall
knowing the sun will return to a cleaner sky.

THE MOMENT BEFORE IMPACT

In the passenger seat, the swerve woke me
from sleep, stripped bare into a mere man who
could only watch the distance close in.
The driver's shriek faded out as I died.
His moans growing louder told me I had
not died. Between dying and not dying was
a blank, an imposed short circuit. The stories lied:
the lifetime reel failed to roll. A child subjected
to parental guidance during the only parts
of a movie that matter can swear by his
impending adultness. But what can one do
with a blank? In the moment before impact,
magnified into milliseconds, I could not
protest against my body locking me out
and releasing me after a crash I can only imagine,
to pick up what is left of my wreckage and drag
myself out to find a safe patch of earth to lie on,
wondering why no one can keep up with
the many ways their body can break,
cursed forever to a blank that contains
the secret of how, precisely, everything broke.

A LIGHT-RAIL THAT DERAILED

Trampled by a stampede of dreams, my brother,
unable to stay laid down, sat on the bed and swung
his feet. Then he stood. Then he paced. His eyes,
swollen, carried the weight of arrears of sleep,
but he would not submit himself. There were things
he must say, truths he must stay awake to relay,
so, I let him speak even though my limited psyche
failed me so that I could not follow him from one thought
to the next. He did not resist the shot that finally knocked
him cold. The doctor called it a *derailment,* and I imagined
my brother, a light-rail, carrying too much to not derail
from his tracks. The hospital never changed each time
I've had to bring him back. The air held every dust in place;
perhaps it knew that, here, too much was already displaced.
In the lobby, I sat beside a patient who sat apart from others,
composed, his disdain clear; disappointed in himself for
being there. The next day, my brother kept talking.
I knew he was trying to show he meant to bother no one,
but I told him I just wanted to sit there and watch TV
with him, but I sat instead worrying that the nurses,
when I'd left, snared just as much at him. I felt him
beside me warring against the words crowded inside
his mouth, some leaking out so that his murmurs came
as persistent jolts. The deranged on the street peeling off
his clothes is only reacting to the heat. My brother knows
the world in ways I may never learn—a light-rail
that sometimes travels too far ahead of us.

EXTENDED INCUBATION

The night is fading, but I do not feel my body
settling into sleep. A man's childhood will not stay

still enough to be buried no matter how deeply he digs.
Just ask Pluto if owning your own moon makes

anyone think you are grand. You are only as good
as what you can ruin, and all I can say is that I want

to let you stay, but I do not recognize what my face
reveals these days. I want to lose myself in the space

between what is gone and what remains. Perhaps
what fades can resurface at will, and I can learn

to keep my nights for myself. Perhaps things fade
not because there's a need to make room.

You are an emptiness getting filled. I can't have
the whole of you at once, I don't have as much room.

CONSIDERING SILENCE

Consider a silence that repels sleep
and flits thoughts through places
it has no business being.

You could stay long in the dark until
you feel your eyes lose their fear and you
begin to see so clearly you wonder

what use light serves anyway. Then you can
watch your shadow set itself loose to graze
in the bounty of your body's corruption.

Who says time, weight, and distance are not
a single quantity leaving a changing room
three different times, three shadows standing

over one another? Blowing with your mouth
can set them apart, hunting dogs combing
the earth for what you claim to have lost.

Pluck an eye and hang it as the sun, let it lead you
through the thicket of these uncertainties,
what has become an unaccomplished silence.

COLLATERAL DAMAGE

I crawl past reeds toward a swamp, with a prayer
that water opens itself up to shelter me. I have not

come to count what remains after the flood that
spares a roof but takes much of the pillars

keeping it up. The brain and the heart—one red
as clay, the other white as salt—know firsthand

our impulse to choose whom to save and who
remains collateral damage, so they will not tell us

for sure which is the real custodian of the last
droplets of a life. The current streaming up

from my country's feet will drown its kidneys
and break its bladder, and when the diaphragm

is breached, the flood will choke its lungs and
leave behind only a clayey sea which chokes fish.

THE FUNCTION OF EYES

You can't unsee yourself now.
Ancestors, motivated by the treacherous
habit of eyes, invented cameras
to corroborate tales already employed
to bully the memory. And when you see
those frozen bits of yourself,
your memory plays back how your eyes
told the tale, how your nerves relayed
the pain, how you simply lie there
waiting for the death of mornings.
Your heart falls, knowing that although
your body had collapsed, it could
rebuild itself. And now, stuck between
mourning what is lost and being
grateful to be able to mourn what is lost,
you shut your windows,
        thinking
not of rain
        but dust.

DYING CHEMICALLY

You will let them kill you, but you'll find
this death is a ticket to nirvana; a cascade
where your dreams, having edited your
memories, crash into one another and slide off,
smoothening cracks in your memory,
glossing over ruins on the portrait of your
imagined future. You are blessed with
an aloneness that is the center of this death.
This is where all known pleasures are pulled down
and the bendiness of memory, like water, manifests.
Water that instead drinks you, keeps you in the safety
of its stomach, so that when you slip back to the sight
of infusion pumps and catheters, when the mask
brings back the funny taste of oxygen, and you hear
the clip on your finger continue to narrate your
physiology to a beeping monitor; even then, when the pain
returns to where you are broken—an undulating stream
that spans in all directions of the world, what remains is
the memory of death and all its exquisite secrets.

HOME IS A HEART THAT FLEES
You can't steal the things that God has given me.
No more pain and no more shame and misery.
—Michael Kiwanuka

I am listening in my head to echoes
of slammed doors. Do not praise me
for my patience, I only know better
than to scream back at a void.

My friends do not stand for the national
anthem because you only imagine
dying for something that loves you,
and the *Pledge* is a vapid poem.

Home is to where the heart flees.
When each of us who bear scars of our
country's stabs sleeps, we fly over
the Atlantic and its siblings into dreams.

I have learned that passion can never
fill in for peace. Home is where you can
shake off what hails you and then fall
into sleep. Here we must lie on infested

beds without sheets, but to go elsewhere
is to be reminded that in a hotel, you can
only be a guest. Perhaps home is
a heart that flees and never sleeps.

I do not want to fight a mob of armed
sheep to walk through my front door.
You can have all I have not been given
but don't you ask what I can give.

ACKNOWLEDGMENTS

"A Bowl of Moonlight" first appeared in *Acumen*.

The last two lines of "Puppy in Love" are adapted from Zadie Smith's *On Beauty*.

"Considering Silence" first appeared in the *Chaffin Journal* as "Mapping Silence."

"My Father Renamed Himself" first appeared in *Efiko*.

"The Statesman" first appeared in the anthology *The Flute: African Urban Echoes*.